NORFOLK BUSES

JOHN LAW

AMBERLEY

First published 2016

Amberley Publishing
The Hill, Stroud
Gloucestershire, GL5 4EP

www.amberley-books.com

Copyright © John Law, 2016

The right of John Law to be identified as
the Author of this work has been asserted in
accordance with the Copyrights, Designs and
Patents Act 1988.

ISBN 978 1 4456 5391 4 (print)
ISBN 978 1 4456 5392 1 (ebook)

British Library Cataloguing in Publication Data.
A catalogue record for this book is available from
the British Library.

Typesetting by Amberley Publishing.
Printed in the UK.

Introduction

Norfolk is largely rural, forming the northern section of East Anglia. The eastern side of the county is dominated by the only city and county town, Norwich. One other large conurbation in the east is around Great Yarmouth, a seaside town and busy port.

The west of Norfolk has only one major town, King's Lynn, close to The Wash and the border with Lincolnshire. There are, of course, several smaller towns: Dereham, Thetford, Wells-next-the-Sea, Cromer, for example.

Until the 1980s, one bus company, Eastern Counties Omnibus Company (ECOC), dominated the entire county. Apart from a few infrequent or market day routes, only three independent bus companies ran stage carriage services within the county. Dack's (trading as Rosemary Coaches) operated several routes into King's Lynn, while Culling's Coaches served villages around Norwich and Simond's of Botesdale ran into the county town from the south.

I first visited Norfolk in the early 1970s, travelling by train from London to Norwich. Exiting Norwich Thorpe station, I was greeted by a fleet of ECOC standardised Bristol buses, bodied by Eastern Coach Works (ECW), a few still in Tilling red, but most had already received National Bus Company all-over red. It would be unfair to criticise the frequency of services at that time, but in the economic climate of the 1970s and 1980s, it was inevitable that cuts were imposed. Once, in Norwich, I had tremendous difficulty in reaching the university from the city centre, mid-evening. I also found it impossible to get from Hunstanton to Wells-next-the-Sea direct, except for I think a Wednesday! Fortunately, things have changed for the better, possibly thanks to the Transport Act of 1985. More of that as you read on.

The history of ECOC reflects that of similar large neighbouring companies, United Counties, Eastern National and Lincolnshire Road Car. All became part of the Tilling Group, which was nationalised in January 1948. In common with the rest of the group, the main intake of buses was from the Bristol Commercial Vehicles factory, another nationalised concern. Most were bodied in Lowestoft by Eastern Coach Works (ECW), another business in the hands of the British Transport Commision. There were some exceptions to the above, especially in earlier days. Even by 1967, a small batch of Bedford VAM buses (bodied by ECW of course!) was delivered to ECOC. It should be pointed out that ECOC did not just serve Norfolk. The company's operations covered virtually all of neighbouring Suffolk and Cambridgeshire.

Another Transport Act, of 1968, saw the formation of the National Bus Company (NBC) on 1 January 1969. All former Tilling companies were included, so ECOC became just another NBC subsidiary, quickly adopting the corporate red livery style. As mentioned, ECOC had a virtual monopoly of Norfolk's bus services, a situation maintained until Margaret Thatcher came to power. Her government introduced deregulation throughout England in 1986. In preparation for this, the Cambridgeshire operations of ECOC were split off to become Cambus in 1984. Similarly ECOC's coach operations became a separate company, Ambassador Travel, based in Great Yarmouth.

Another part of government policy was to sell off the National Bus Company to private investors. Accordingly, in 1987, an Eastern Counties management buyout occurred, with a new red and yellow colour scheme being introduced. Vehicle purchasing policy had already changed by then.

Like other British operators, minibuses had been introduced. The new management continued this, but also invested in larger buses, including some from Dennis and other manufacturers.

In 1994, ECOC passed into the hands of the GRT Group, which soon became part of First Group, who retain ownership today. In 1996, First Group also purchased Norfolk's only council-owned bus operation, Great Yarmouth Transport. The blue colour scheme was adopted to match First's livery style, but like ECOC itself, First's 'Barbie' stripes soon took over.

Let us now look at independent operations in Norfolk. As already mentioned, Culling's (also known as Red Car Service) ran two rural services from a base in central Norwich but went into liquidation in 1981. In contrast, the other small company running stage carriage services was a Suffolk concern, Simond's of Botesdale, still operating today. Simond's main stage carriage service ran from Bury St Edmunds, calling at Diss (where a depot was maintained) en route. When I first came across this fine operator I was lucky enough to travel on a rare Commer-Harrington, ex-Maidstone and District.

In West Norfolk, ECOC's monopoly was broken by Rosemary Coaches (Dack's), who ran several routes out of King's Lynn. The company had a fascinating fleet, based at Terrington St Clement, with the former Doughty's yard in King's Lynn being used during the 1980s. ECOC took over in the mid-1990s.

Many smaller operators ran infrequent or market day services into King's Lynn. Tuesday was always a good day to visit the town, as the parking area in the bus station was always full of a variety of buses and coaches, from all over Norfolk, Cambridgeshire and Lincolnshire. Examples were CS Pegg of Caston, Coach Services of Thetford and Eagles of Castle Acre.

A relative newcomer to the King's Lynn bus scene was Norfolk Green, who commenced bus services in 1996. The company rapidly expanded and vastly improved frequencies along the north Norfolk coast, at one time with a 30-minute frequency from Hunstanton to Wells-next-the-Sea and onwards towards Cromer. Norfolk Green even reached the city of Norwich. So successful was Norfolk Green that First Group sold their North West Norfolk operations to them in April 2011. However, in December 2013, Norfolk Green was taken over by the Stagecoach Group. For a while, operations were kept separate and a revised green livery was retained. Today though, standard Stagecoach colours are now applied. Recently, competition has returned to the King's Lynn to Hunstanton corridor, with Lynxbus running a small fleet of Optare Tempo single-deckers.

Independent operators have expanded greatly in Norwich and North East Norfolk since deregulation. Even before 1986, Norfolk Bluebird began city services in Norwich, though these didn't last too long. Anglian Buses, originally based in Loddon, now operate lots of routes around Norwich and the Suffolk border, though the company is now a subsidiary of the Go Ahead Group. The same fate befell Konectbus of Dereham, who still run several local services in that area, plus Norwich park-and-ride duties.

Park-and-ride is now important to the citizens of Norwich. At one time, Ambassador Travel and Norfolk County Council operated some of these, but a large proportion of them were, until recently, in the hands of First Bus and Norse. At the time of writing, all are now run by Konectbus.

One large bus company remaining independent is Sanders of Holt, who now have a large hold on the routes to the north of Norwich, including the coastal town of Cromer and Sheringham. Naturally, there are several other small bus companies running around rural Norfolk, too numerous to mention here, but some are illustrated within these pages.

I hope you enjoy my portrayal of the Norfolk bus scene from the early 1970s until the present day.

Finally, I must thank my good friends Richard Huggins and Hugh Madgin for providing a few photographs to cover some gaps in my own collection. I must also show my appreciation to those good people that operate *Bus Lists on the Web*, an internet site that saved me endless trawling through paper fleet lists during the production of this book.

We start the story of Eastern Counties in the early 1970s, with a Bristol LH6P/ECW bus of 1970 vintage, still in the old Tilling style pre-National Bus Company colour scheme. Fleet number LH902 (XPW 902H) is seen in London Road, in the outskirts of King's Lynn.

An earlier style of Eastern Counties livery is demonstrated here on this preserved bus, attending a rally in King's Lynn in 1981. 1950-built Bristol LSX4G/ECW forty-two-seater LL744 (MAH 744) was the second prototype LS-type chassis built. It now resides in the Ipswich Transport Museum.

One of the oldest vehicles in the 1970s Eastern Counties fleet was this 1949 Bristol L6B departmental tree-lopper and towing lorry. Originally fleet number LS495 (GPW 495), it carried a Beadle coach body. In its rebuilt form, numbered X42, it is seen in the old Norwich bus station and depot complex, *c.* 1975.

Sometime around 1974, Eastern Counties LS804 (3804 PW) is seen on a stage service in Great Yarmouth. Built in 1962, this Bristol MW6G was built as a thirty-two-seat ECW bodied coach, but is seen here downgraded to bus duties and painted in all-over red livery.

Typical of the Eastern Counties fleet of the mid-1970s are these two Bristol MW6G single-deckers, seen in Norwich bus station, *c.* 1975. On the left is LM604 (AAH 911B), built in 1964, with forty-five-seat bus bodywork, with the rather uninformative 'SERVICE' as a destination. To its right is LS820 (820 BNG), this time a thirty-nine-seat coach, built in 1962, looking rather smart in National Bus Company white coaching livery, though it looks to be on a local bus service.

Eastern Counties Bristol MW6G/ECW forty-five-seat bus, number LM978 (478 BPW) is photographed close to the railway station in Sheringham, on the North Norfolk coast. It is about to depart on a journey to Norwich, *c.* 1975.

Norfolk Buses

Several National Bus Company operators suffered from bus shortages during the mid-1970s, with Eastern Counties being no exception. Seen in Norwich, on hire from Suffolk operator Partridge of Hadleigh, is FVO 71D, a Bedford VAM5/Plaxton forty-five-seat coach. This coach was new to Barton Transport, a large Nottinghamshire concern, who would have used it on stage carriage duties. In this photo, it is doing just that, as it passes the Canary Football Pools offices.

In 1967, Eastern Counties purchased a small batch of non-standard buses, though with ECW bodies. This unusual combination is seen in King's Lynn bus station's layover area, *c.* 1975. Number SB663 (NAH 663F) is a Bedford VAM14, seating forty-one. After sale in 1976, it saw further service with a Bedfordshire school.

Norwich bus station was situated alongside an Eastern Counties depot and so it was possible to take a peek inside. On an occasion, possibly 1975, we see Bristol RELH6G/ECW forty-seven-seat coach, number RE663 (HAH 893D), sharing the garage with a Bristol FS double-decker and a Bristol RE saloon.

Another Eastern Counties vehicle in National white livery here, this time with the bus style of ECW bodywork, though to dual-purpose standard, seating forty-nine passengers. Fleet number RLE743 (GCL 345N), a 1974-built Bristol RELH6L, is seen in Norwich bus station, *c.* 1977.

Eastern Counties' NBC-style dual-purpose red and white colours are seen here applied to 1970-built Bristol RELL6G/ECW fifty-seater, number RLE862 (WNG 862H). The location is Norwich bus station again, in 1981.

A most unusual bus here, on loan to Eastern Counties. CWO 600K is a Leyland FG900/ Willowbrook battery-electric bus, built for evaluation by the Department of the Environment. It seated just nine passengers and the battery life was only four hours or so, therefore it was not considered to be a great success. It is photographed outside Norwich Thorpe station in 1973.

We are back at King's Lynn bus station again, sometime around 1976. Eastern Counties LH696 (VAH 696H) is laying over, prior to working a local route. This Bristol LH6P is one carrying the earlier design of ECW forty-five-seat bodywork, without the later curved windscreen.

A 1978-built Bristol LH6L/ECW B43F, with curved windscreen, is seen inside Norwich city centre depot. Fleet number LH929 (WEX 929S) was found alongside a Bristol FLF double-decker and some Leyland Leopard coaches in 1981.

Passing BT's road works on one side of Caister Road and the Great Yarmouth Transport depot on the other, is Eastern Counties FLF423 (MVX 883C), an ex-Eastern National Bristol FLF6G of 1965 vintage, carrying an ECW H38/32F body. It was transferred to Eastern Counties in 1973 and is seen in 1981, towards the end of its life.

Another second-hand double-decker bus in the Eastern Counties fleet, which received an extension to its normal life by virtue of being converted to open-top. OT1 (VDV 752) was new to Western National in 1957. Eastern Counties bought it in 1979. The Bristol LDL6G/ECW O37/33R is seen in Sheringham on Seaside Special duties in 1981.

Like most other National Bus Company subsidiaries, Eastern Counties received several batches of integral Leyland National saloons. LN593 (WAH 593S) is a fifty-three-seat bus, seen inside Norwich city centre depot in March 1981.In 1993 it received a rebuild by East Lancs, to the Greenway specification, for further service with Eastern Counties.

The Workington factory making the Leyland National revamped the design of the bus, introducing the Leyland National 2 in 1979. Eastern Counties number LN608 (KVG 608V), built in 1980, seating forty-nine passengers, is seen on Prince of Wales Road, Norwich, having just passed Thorpe railway station, in May 1981.

A view of Eastern Counties' Aylsham yard, taken by Richard Huggins on 11 August 1984. On the left is a standard Leyland National 2, number LN602 (KVG 602V), while in the centre is similar LG781 (DPW 781T), refitted with a Gardner engine. On the right is VR149 (GNG 715N), a Bristol VRT/SL6G with the usual ECW bodywork.

Captured on film outside King's Lynn railway station on a sunny day in 1982 is Eastern Counties number LL828 (WEX 828X). This almost new Leyland Leopard, with stylish ECW forty-seven-seat coachwork, is painted in a version of British Rail's livery. It is waiting to depart on the Rail Link express service to Wisbech and Peterborough. Today this service is operated by First Bus and runs, every 30 minutes, as the X1 between Peterborough and Lowestoft, via King's Lynn, Norwich and Great Yarmouth.

Eastern Counties had a large fleet of standard-height Bristol VR double-deckers, but here is an exception to the rule. HVR334 (KKE 734N) is an ex-Maidstone and District Bristol VRT/SL6G of 1975, with high bridge ECW seventy-seven-seat bodywork. Painted in an unusual version of NBC red livery, it is seen in Tombland, Norwich, November 1986.

One of many of the marque ordered by Eastern Counties is number VR160 (JNG 58N), a Bristol VRT/SL6G, built in 1975, with normal ECW bodywork. The bus is seen through the camera of Richard Huggins, who photographed it on the A149 in Sheringham, 2 August 1986.

During the summer of 1986, British Rail rebuilt the River Wensum swing bridge on the approach to Norwich Thorpe station, denying access to the city for trains from Ely and London. Accordingly, the long-closed station at Trowse, on the outskirts of the city, was temporarily reopened. Eastern Counties ran the connecting bus service between the two terminals. Waiting for passengers outside Trowse station is number VR217 (BCL 217T), a 1978-built Bristol VRT/SL3/6LXB, bodied, as usual, by ECW. Richard Huggins photographed this scene on 3 August 1986.

The North Norfolk coast is a well-known seaside holiday area, where open-top buses are popular in high summer. On such duties is former Ribble Motor Service 1980 (NCK 980J), a 1971 Bristol VRT/SL6G with ECW body. De-roofed and renumbered OT4 with Eastern Counties, Richard Huggins photographed the bus at Sheringham station, 2 August 1986. Open-top bus services are still operated in the area, in the hands of Sanders of Holt.

Eastern Counties was not immune to the minibus revolution of the mid- to late 1980s. A precursor to this was Docking Community Bus – the operation of occasional services in the area to the north-east of King's Lynn. Bought specifically for these routes, Ford Transit MB993 (A993 LVG), converted to a sixteen-seater by Mellor, is seen in King's Lynn bus station in the spring of 1985.

Another sixteen-seat Ford Transit minibus, a Dormobile conversion this time, fleet number MB962 (C962 YAH) in the Eastern Counties fleet. It is seen departing Thorpe station, on a Norwich local service, November 1986.

I have been unable to find the full details of this 1985-built Ford Transit minibus in the Eastern Counties fleet. Given the Norfolk registration, it must have been bought new by the company. C410 AEX is lettered for the National Norfolk Community Bus operations. Richard Huggins photographed it close to the long-closed Tivetshall railway station on 4 January 1986.

Eastern Counties, like most operators, soon found a source of larger minibuses during the early 1990s. Number MB45 (L245 PAH) in the fleet was a 1993-built Mercedes 609D, with bodywork by Frank Guy, seating twenty passengers. It is seen in Castle Meadow, central Norwich, in early 1994, on a city service.

MB745 (C745 BEX) was delivered to Eastern Counties in May 1986. This Mercedes L608D, with Reeve Burgess twenty-seat bodywork is seen in Norwich bus station in November 1986 on a local city route.

Privatisation soon saw new orders for larger buses enter into the Eastern Counties fleet. DD1 (F101 AVG) was one of the first delivered, in 1989. Only a year old, the Northern Counties-bodied Leyland Olympian is seen passing Norwich Thorpe railway station, heading into the city, summer 1990.

YFY 5M was a dual-doored Leyland National, new to Southport Corporation, just before Merseyside PTE took over. In 1994, East Lancs rebuilt it as a fifty-two-seater, to Greenway specification, for Eastern Counties. Given fleet number 667, it is seen in green park-and-ride livery, Castle Meadow, Norwich, early 1996.

New to Eastern Counties in late 1992, for park-and-ride duties, was this Dennis Dart/Plaxton combination. Number S42 (K742 JAH) was seen in Norwich bus station, temporarily out of service, in 1993.

Here is Eastern Counties number DD23 (J623 BVG), a 1991-built Leyland Olympian, bodied by Leyland itself. Very much a standard double-decker of the time, it is seen in central Norwich, in February 1993.

Eastern Counties ordered a few Dennis Javelins around the end of the 1980s. Some had coachwork built in Wigan by Northern Counties, but this example, number S8 (G708 JAH), carries a Duple 300 body, to dual-purpose specification, seating forty-eight passengers. It is seen in Norwich bus station in early 1994, ready to depart for Loddon.

It is perhaps appropriate that we take a look at Great Yarmouth Transport at this stage, as the former council-owned company was taken over by First Group in 1996 and absorbed into the Eastern Counties fleet. A varied collection of buses was operated in the town, all bearing a blue livery. Number 3 (DEX 703) was one of several Leyland Atlantean PDR1/1 double-deckers, this one built in 1960. With Metro-Cammell bodywork, it is seen near to the depot on Caister Road, *c.* 1978.

Here is another Leyland Atlantean PDR1/1, number 6 (AEX 26B), manufactured in 1964 and given Leeds-built Roe bodywork. It is seen inside the main depot in 1981.

Great Yarmouth Corporation also had a sizeable amount of single-decker buses. Typical of the fleet purchased in the mid-1960s is number 86 (AEX 86B), photographed just after it had crossed the River Yare and entered the town centre. This short AEC Reliance was unusual in that it carried a thirty-nine-seat Pennine body.

Great Yarmouth Corporation received an even rarer chassis/body combination in 1964. Here is number 19 (AEX 19B), out of use in the depot yard in 1977. This Daimler Freeline was fitted with a Roe forty-five-seat dual-purpose body. It is shown carrying the name Rambouillet, a commune near Paris and a twin town of Great Yarmouth. The Daimler Freeline was not a popular bus with most operators, but this one lasted a good few years in Norfolk.

A batch of Daimler Fleetline double-deckers was also ordered for service in Great Yarmouth. One of these, number 53 (HEX 253), with Roe bodywork, is seen on a dull day in the town centre, *c.* 1975.

The Leyland Atlantean was normally a rear-engined double-decker bus, but Great Yarmouth purchased a batch of three Marshall, thirty-nine-seat bodied PDR1/1 single-decker examples. Representing this unusual combination is number 42 (GEX 742F), posed outside the depot in 1977.

Painted in a rather garish livery to celebrate the Queen's Silver Jubilee is Great Yarmouth Transport number 10 (FEX 110). This 30-foot-long Daimler CVG6, with Roe seventy-three-seat bodywork, is seen in the depot yard, 1977.

During the 1970s, the majority of the Great Yarmouth fleet was formed of AEC Swift single-deckers. After the demise of the neighbouring Lowestoft's Waveney District Council bus operation, a few more were added to the fleet. Number 91 (NRT564L), with ECW dual-doored forty-five-seat bodywork, is seen inside the depot in 1981. It was previously number 17 in the Waveney fleet.

Here is another ECW-bodied AEC Swift in the Great Yarmouth Transport fleet. Number 81 (WEX 681M) was bought new in 1973, seating forty-three passengers in its dual-doored bodywork. It is seen in the town centre in 1976. In the background to the left is the tower of the Minster Church of Saint Nicholas.

The earliest batch of AEC Swifts carried Willowbrook dual-doored bodywork, again seating forty-three passengers. Number 62 (LEX862H) is seen in Great Yarmouth town centre, 1976.

In 1977, Great Yarmouth Transport turned back to double-decker buses for its operations. On the edge of the town centre, passing a long-gone café and a Tolly Cobbold pub, is number 35 (RVF 35R), sometime around 1978. The bus is a seventy-seven-seat Bristol VRTSL6G with ECW bodywork, built in nearby Lowestoft.

Posed outside the iconic depot frontage of Great Yarmouth Transport is fleet number 63 (K63 KEX), an East Lancashire-bodied Dennis Dart with forty-three dual-purpose seats. New in 1993, it was photographed in early 1996.

Great Yarmouth Transport number 44 (E44 OAH) was a MCW Metrorider twenty-five-seater, built to dual-purpose specification. It was photographed outside Yarmouth Vauxhall railway station on a wet day in January 1988.

The late 1980s saw the construction of a new bus station in Great Yarmouth, part of a shopping complex in the town centre. Leaving the darkness of the terminal is GYT fleet number 58 (G458 KNG), a Dennis Dart/Carlyle B39F, built in 1990 and seen in the summer of that year.

It is a beautifully sunny day in the summer of 1990 and Great Yarmouth Transport number 41 (E41 OAH) is seen in Gorleston town centre. Fitted with seventy-eight coach seats, the vehicle is a 1987 Volvo B10M-50 Citybus, bodied by East Lancashire.

Great Yarmouth Transport was not immune to the minibus revolution, as illustrated by fleet number 53 (G53 GEX). Bearing Blue Buses on its front, it is a 1989-built Mercedes 811D with Reeve Burgess DP33F bodywork. Like the top photograph, it is the summer of 1990, in Gorleston.

When First Group took over Great Yarmouth Transport, they integrated the fleet with that of First Eastern Counties, though retaining the Blue Buses identity and adopting a blue and cream colour scheme. Brought in from the main ECOC fleet, number 615 (PEX 615W) is seen in its new guise as it departs from Great Yarmouth's bus station in autumn 1997. This Leyland National 2 was new in 1980 and had the capacity for forty-nine seated passengers.

Painted in the same livery style as the above bus is First Blue Bus number 329 (CVF 29T). This 1979 Bristol VRT/SL3/6LXB with ECW bodywork was new as Great Yarmouth Transport number 29. It is seen in its hometown, leaving the bus station and passing Wetherspoon's Troll Cart pub in autumn 1997.

Number 104 (F101 AVG) in the First Blue Bus fleet is seen departing Great Yarmouth bus station, again in autumn 1997. New to Eastern Counties as DD1 in 1989, this Leyland Olympian has Northern Counties' seventy-five-seat bodywork.

Transferred into the Great Yarmouth operation of First Blue Bus from a neighbouring subsidiary, Eastern National, is number 411 (L807 OPU). This 1994-built Dennis Dart/Plaxton B34F bus is seen departing Great Yarmouth bus station for Caister again in autumn 1997.

We now turn back to the main Eastern Counties fleet, just after the First Group takeover. For several years, the old livery and fleetnames were retained, along with the First logo, seen clearly on number 76 (G125 YEV) in Norwich bus station, November 2000. This 1989 Leyland Olympian/Alexander double-decker was new to Ensign of Purfleet, Essex. A former London Dennis Dart/Wright saloon can be seen on the left.

A brighter version of First Eastern Counties livery is seen applied to number 283 (VEX 283X), a standard Bristol VRT/SL3/6LXB with seventy-four-seat ECW body. It is photographed on a sunny day in King's Lynn bus station layover area, *c.* 1999.

Another standard Bristol VRT/SL3/6LXB with ECW bodywork in the current First Eastern Counties colour scheme of the time, but this one was a second-hand purchase. New to Trent Motor Traction in 1981, as number 854 (PRC 854X), it is seen in central Norwich in the autumn of 1997 as Eastern Counties number 308.

Transferred in from another First Bus subsidiary, Northampton Transport, is this Bristol VRT/SL3/6LXB of 1981 vintage, fitted with East Lancashire bodywork. Given fleet number 336, ABD 72X is seen without a First Bus logo, in central Norwich, March 1996.

Here we have another transferred bus from within the First Group. Eastern Counties number 69 (G48 XLO), a 1989-built Leyland Olympian/Alexander, is seen in Norwich bus station, September 2001. It was new to London Buslines, for whom it operated in the western suburbs of the capital.

On the western side of the county, seen departing from King's Lynn bus station in the spring of 1997, is First Eastern Counties number 955 (G615 GAH). This is a 1995-built Mercedes 609D minibus, adopted for bus use by Frank Guy, seating twenty passengers.

Number 455 (M202 VWW) in the First Eastern Counties fleet is seen in King's Lynn bus station in the summer of 1999. This 1995 Dennis Dart/Plaxton forty-seater was transferred from First Group subsidiary Yorkshire Rider.

Originally Eastern Counties fleet number LN781, DPW 781T, is seen in King's Lynn, again in 1999. This forty-nine-seat Leyland National 2 has now been renumbered 651 and it has received a Gardner engine, like several in the fleet.

First Eastern Counties Excel X94 limited stop route was the successor to the British Rail-sponsored service between Peterborough and King's Lynn (see page 14). Coach number 34 (P734 NVG) is seen in its dedicated livery, showing the route as running every two hours between Peterborough and Norwich, though its destination is Great Yarmouth. The X94 was later replaced by the X1, running every 30 minutes through the day. The vehicle, a Plaxton bodied Volvo B10M-62, was photographed while pausing its journey in King's Lynn bus station, *c.* 1999.

At the same spot as above, heading in the opposite direction, in April 2003, is First Eastern Counties number 202 (AO02 RBZ). Demonstrating the corporate First Bus livery for the X94, the coach is another Volvo/Plaxton fifty-three-seater, albeit in the latest style.

The low-floor bus has arrived in the First Eastern Counties fleet and First Group's 'Barbie' livery has been applied. When newly introduced, this colour scheme was only applied to new buses, but it would soon be seen throughout the country. Fleet number 481 (R681 DPW), a 1998-built Dennis Dart SLF with Plaxton thirty-seven-seat bodywork, is at King's Lynn bus station in 1999.

Also in First's corporate colours is another low-floor bus. Number 576 (T576 JNG), a Scania L94UB with Wright forty-seat body, is found in King's Lynn bus station in 1999, when the bus was almost new. It will soon depart for Hunstanton, via Sandringham, a route later lost to Norfolk Green.

First Group later adopted a national five-figure numbering scheme and dropped the Eastern Counties fleet name from display, though the legal lettering retained it. Number 47250 (M250 VWW), a Dennis Dart with forty-seat Alexander bodywork is seen in Castle Meadow, 2 April 2009. This bus was new to Yorkshire Rider, the main Leeds operator, which was taken over by First Group.

Another transfer from the Yorkshire Rider fleet, First Group number 30886 (W741 DWX) has reached King's Lynn bus station, 10 November 2010. This low-floor double-decker is a 2000-built Volvo B7TL-57 with Alexander bodywork.

As we have already seen, First Group's Eastern Counties operation was no stranger to transfers from other members of the organisation. This bus, photographed in King's Lynn on 10 November 2010, was new to Western National. Number 42429 (P429 ORL) is a standard Dennis Dart SLF, of 1996 vintage, with Plaxton thirty-five-seat bus bodywork.

This thirty-seat Optare Solo midibus, number 53121 (EO02 NFC), was new to fellow First Group operator Essex Buses in May 2002. It is seen in central Norwich, crossing the River Wensum on Wensum Street, 29 March 2012.

Most Norwich city services still use Castle Meadow, but long distance and park-and-ride routes use the impressive new bus station, opened in 2005. This forms the backdrop to First Group number 32483 (AU53 HKA), a Volvo B7TL/Alexander double-decker, on a council-sponsored park-and-ride service on 2 April 2009.

First Group's cascaded buses from London operate several Norwich city routes. New to Centrewest, one of First's capital operations, number 33239 (LT52 WVH) is seen in Norwich city centre, crossing the River Wensum on 29 March 2012. This 2002-built Dennis Trident, with Plaxton body, was originally dual-doored, but was converted to single-door for its East Anglian duties.

Not all buses in Norwich owned by First Group are cascaded from other subsidiaries. Number 36170 (BD11 CFP) was new to the Eastern Counties operation. This Volvo B9TL, with Wright bodywork, seating seventy-six, is seen crossing the River Wensum, on Prince of Wales Road, outside Norwich Thorpe railway station, 16 April 2014.

Similar buses to the one above are now used on the regular X1 Excel service between Peterborough and Lowestoft, via Wisbech, King's Lynn, Swaffham, Norwich and Great Yarmouth. Number 37579 (AU58 EDK), a Volvo B9TL/Wright, with high-backed seats, is calling at King's Lynn bus station, en route for the coast, 24 September 2012.

A look now at an independent that was swallowed up by First Group in 1998. Halesworth Transit began running local services in Great Yarmouth in 1989, trading under the name Flying Banana. Appropriately, a yellow livery was employed, as depicted on this Ford Transit C431 BHY. This sixteen-seat minibus, a Dormobile-bodied example, is seen in Great Yarmouth's bus station in the summer of 1990. The bus was new to the Bristol Omnibus Company.

Halesworth Transit bought N589 WND new for its Great Yarmouth operations. Photographed leaving the bus station in the autumn of 1997, it is a Mercedes 709D with Alexander twenty-seven-seat bodywork.

Back in 1984, Eastern Counties' coaching operations were split from the main company, to form Ambassador Travel. In January 1988, at the small depot-cum-coach station in Great Yarmouth we see number 918 (C918 BPW), an MCW Metroliner double-deck coach seating seventy-one passengers. It is painted in National Express colours, but soon after this photograph was taken, the firm (now in private hands) began concentrating on local bus services.

Ambassador Travel's locally registered HCL 957Y is photographed in Great Yarmouth bus station, in an all-over green colour scheme. The origins of this vehicle are uncertain, as it has been re-registered at least twice! It is known to be a Leyland Tiger with ECW coach bodywork, though it is being used on stage carriage work in late 1997.

Bought new by Ambassador Travel for park-and-ride duties in Norwich was L71 UNG, a Volvo B6 with forty-one-seat Alexander Dash bodywork. It is seen in central Norwich, about to depart for the airport park-and-ride site in late 1994.

On the same duties is Ambassador Travel's L938 ORC, a Mercedes 811D with bodywork by Plaxton, seating thirty-one passengers. Again, this bus was bought new and was found in central Norwich in late 1994.

Norse, a management company working on behalf of Norfolk County Council, operated several of the Norwich park-and-ride services, until 2015, when all of these passed to Go Ahead Group's Konectbus subsidiary. Norse-owned ex-Go Ahead London General Dennis Trident/Plaxton PN03 ULV is seen at Castle Meadow, Norwich, 16 April 2014.

Norse's sister vehicle, PN03 ULT, is seen on the same day as above, again in Castle Meadow. It is painted in a special livery for the airport park-and-ride service.

Dack's, trading as Rosemary Coaches (though not all vehicles carried this name), was an independent operator based at Terrington St Clement, near the border with Lincolnshire, west of King's Lynn. The company ran several stage carriage services around the area, until selling out to First Eastern Counties in the 1990s. In 1974, Leyland Tiger Cub/Plaxton Highway forty-five-seater bus, 531 GUP, was photographed awaiting its next duty in King's Lynn bus station. It was new in 1960 to Armstrong of Ebchester, County Durham.

Here is a view of Dack's depot yard at Terrington St Clement, *c.* 1974. Closest to the camera is 60 BUA, an ex-Wallace Arnold of Leeds 1962 Leyland Leopard. Unusually, it has centre-entrance Plaxton coachwork, so was used mainly on schools services. Several former Barton of Nottingham buses are seen in the background.

Seen at the back of the previous photo, VUP 742 is a 1957-built Leyland Tiger Cub, with Burlingham forty-five-seat bus bodywork. This was new to another County Durham independent, The Eden of West Auckland.

Another of Dack's coaches is seen laying over between schools duties in King's Lynn coach park, *c.* 1974. Registered DJP 346, this Leyland Tiger Cub, of 1958, with Plaxton forty-one-seat coachwork, was new to well-known coach operator, Smiths of Wigan.

Not all of Dack's buses received a repaint prior to entering service. An example, photographed in the mid-1970s, is seen in King's Lynn. 903 LRR still wears the colours of its former operator, Barton of Chilwell, Nottingham. The chassis of this vehicle was once a Leyland PD2/1 registered HD7836, new to Yorkshire Woollen District in 1948. Barton rebuilt the chassis in 1961 and fitted a new full-fronted Northern Counties body. A long-lived bus indeed!

Dack's depot and yard at Terrington St Clement was, as we have seen from some of the previous photos, rather tight for space. The driver of 647 GWP is patiently waiting for a space to become available, taking an opportunity to look at his newspaper, sometime around 1978. This coach, bought from Black and White of Harvington, Worcestershire, is a fine AEC Reliance with Duple Alpine Continental bodywork.

Dack's later took over the old Doughty's yard in the outskirts of King's Lynn. It is here that we see EUF 197D, a former Southdown Leyland Leopard with Plaxton forty-nine-seat coachwork, the photograph dating to around 1979.

New to another South-Eastern BET operator, FKL 131D was originally fleet number C68 in the Maidstone & District fleet. Bought by Dack's in 1978, it is a Harrington-bodied forty-seven-seat AEC Reliance of 1966, photographed in King's Lynn bus station, March 1980.

Still in the livery of a previous operator, DJW 278C was new as a demonstrator in 1965. This AEC Reliance had unusual Strachans forty-nine-seat dual-purpose bodywork. It is seen with Dack's in King's Lynn bus station in spring 1978.

In full Dack's colours, though without fleet names, JRC 259D is seen in the sun at King's Lynn in 1982. This Leyland Leopard with Metro-Cammell firty-one-seat body was new to Trent Motor Traction as fleet number 259 in 1966 and was bought by Dack's in 1979.

Dack's purchased second-hand vehicles from a variety of sources. JPA 166K was originally number RP66 in the London Country Bus Services fleet, where it was used on Green Line express duties. This AEC Reliance has Park Royal dual-purpose coachwork, seating forty-five passengers, and is seen in King's Lynn depot yard in 1981.

In a slightly varied colour scheme, Dack's-owned JHW 62E was found in King's Lynn yard in 1981. New to Bristol Omnibus Company in 1967, given fleet number C7294, this Bristol FLF6B has ECW seventy-seat bodywork.

Another former Maidstone & District coach in the Dack's fleet. New in 1968, NKL 210F is a Duple-bodied Leyland Leopard seating forty-five passengers. It is seen in King's Lynn in 1981.

GVW 981H in the Dack's fleet is seen through Richard Huggins's camera lens at the site of the long closed Yarmouth Beach railway station on 11 November 1984. This coach, new to Eastern National, is a Bristol RELH6G with forty-two-seat ECW bodywork.

A rather unusual coach in the Dack's fleet was NAG 115G, seen at King's Lynn depot on 24 September 1983. New to Scottish Bus Group subsidiary Western SMT, for motorway duties, it is a Bristol REMH6G with Alexander forty-two-seat coachwork. Both fleetnames are clearly displayed. Photograph by Richard Huggins.

One of the last buses bought by the Rosemary Coaches (Dack's) business was CKC 302L. This was new to Merseyside Passenger Transport Executive as number 3002 in 1973, for its Wirral operations. Photographed in King's Lynn bus station in mid-1992, it is a Daimler Fleetline with MCW seventy-five-seat bodywork.

As mentioned earlier, the yard used by Dack's in King's Lynn was originally in the hands of Doughty's Coaches. This company once ran stage services, but by the time this photograph was taken, in the spring of 1978, these had ceased. Closest to the camera is YJG 820, a former East Kent Road Car Company 1962 AEC Regent V with rather functional-looking Park Royal bodywork. Alongside, in the depot yard, is a pair of Duple coaches.

Market days in King's Lynn have long attracted the smaller operators of Norfolk and the surrounding areas. Two visitors are seen here, in the bus station, in the summer of 1999. On the left is the Docking Community Bus, run by West Norfolk County Council, in the form of Mercedes minibus P760 OCL. Alongside is a visitor from Littleport, Cambridgeshire, a Bova coach, with 'cherished' registration, 227 ASV, owned by Storeys Coaches.

Eagles, from the Norfolk village of Castle Acre, ran into King's Lynn, bringing market day shoppers into the town. This smart coach, PRO 447W, a 1980-built Bedford YMT with Duple Dominant body, new to Sonner of Gillingham, Kent, is seen in King's Lynn bus station in summer, 1999.

The small West Norfolk village of Wormegay, mentioned in the Domesday Book, is best known for its motte-and-bailey castle. Wormegay was also the home of Harrod's Coaches, though the company has now moved to nearby Downham Market. Like many coaching businesses, a market day run into King's Lynn is part of its operations. On such duties is OHE 282X, a Leyland Tiger/Plaxton coach, new to National Travel East. It is seen in King's Lynn bus station, summer 1999.

Caroline Seagull Coaches was a Great Yarmouth-based operator, with a good variety of buses and coaches. The company was run from a small depot, at Queen's Road near the town centre, and from a yard in Cobholm, to the south of the town. At the former, in 1977, is 902 FUP, a 1960-built AEC Reliance, with Roe forty-five-seat bodywork. This bus was new to Economic of Whitburn and was once a regular performer on the South Shields to Sunderland route.

Caroline Seagull Coaches once operated tours of their seaside hometown. Purchased for these duties was JSC 890E, a Leyland Atlantean PDR1/1 with Alexander bodywork, new to Edinburgh Corporation. It was later converted to open-top, as seen here outside Queen's Road depot in 1990.

Caroline Seagull certainly liked their AEC Reliance coaches and purchased a varied selection from several sources. 824 BWN, seen in Queen's Road in 1977, was new to South Wales Transport. This coach had a classic thrity-seven-seat Harrington body.

Purchased from East Kent in 1979, GJG 641D was a 1966 AEC Reliance, with unusual Park Royal forty-nine-seat coach body. It is seen in the Cobholm yard, lettered for bingo duties, in late 1983.

A sunny day in late 1989 sees us at the Cobholm yard of Caroline Seagull Coaches, with a variety of vehicles on display. The main subject of this photograph, BPT 670L, is a Leyland Leopard with Plaxton Elite Express coachwork. This fifty-one-seater was new to North East operator Trimdon Motor Services in 1973. Also seen are ex-East Kent rebuilt AEC Reliance 537 FN and GEX 632Y, a Bedford YNT/Plaxton coach bought new.

On the same occasion as above, another AEC Reliance is seen in the Cobholm yard. SCM 100K carries Plaxton Elite coachwork. Carrying fifty-three passengers, this vehicle was new to Harding's (Selwyn's) of Birkenhead in 1972. Caroline Seagull Coaches ceased trading in 2008.

Alongside their service buses, Culling's had an interesting coach fleet. One of the oldest of these is seen in the Norwich depot yard, *c.* 1975. XDV 850 is an AEC Reliance, with Willowbrook forty-one-seat coachwork. It was new as fleet number TCR850 to Devon General in 1958.

Culling's, also trading as Red Car Services, ran a couple of rural routes using buses based at a small depot in Ber Street, central Norwich. At that location, sometime in 1981, Bedford YRQ/Willowbrook fifty-two-seat bus UCL 826K awaits its next duty. This bus was bought new by Culling's for their stage carriage workings.

Another view at Culling's Norwich depot in 1981, though on a different occasion. A pair of ex-East Kent AEC Reliances is ready and waiting for departure on two rural services. Both OFN 714F and OFN 730F have Marshall fifty-three-seat bodywork, built in 1968.

One of the more unusual vehicles in the Culling's fleet was GEX 257N, an AEC Reliance with a Willowbrook 002 body, fitted with fifty-one coach seats. It is seen on excursion duties in central Norwich, *c.* 1976.

Bedford chassis types were also favoured by Culling's. Bought new was PPW 800F, a 1968-built VAM70, with Plaxton Panorama forty-five-seat coachwork. It is seen at Norwich depot on a sunny day, *c.* 1977, looking slightly battered and relegated to squash club duties.

On the same occasion as above, a second-hand AEC Reliance coach is seen in the depot yard. ROE 705G was constructed in 1969 for Bowen of Birmingham. Fitted with forty-nine-seat Plaxton Elite coachwork, it was purchased by Culling's in 1976.

Though full deregulation of Britain's bus services was introduced in 1986, prior to that it became possible, under certain circumstances, for a limited amount of competition to be commenced. A firm named Norfolk Bluebird took advantage of this, running buses in Norwich. On such duties is SMU 726N, a 1974 Daimler Fleetline with MCW body. New as London Transport number DM1726, the bus is seen in central Norwich in spring 1985.

On the same occasion, below the mound supporting Norwich Castle, we see Norfolk Bluebird coach EHW 314K. New to Bristol Omnibus Company in 1972, this is a Bristol RELH6G with Plaxton coachwork. It was standard practice with Norfolk Bluebird to only use paper destination indicators, as seen behind the vehicle's windscreen. The company's bus routes did not last very long.

Simond's, a Suffolk operator, based in Botesdale, has long operated a Bury St Edmunds to Norwich service. A depot is maintained in the small Norfolk town of Diss, between the two locations. Seen in Diss, on 6 July 1974, is UKN 203. This is a rare example of a 1955-built Commer-Harrington integral bus, seating forty-two passengers. It was new to Maidstone and District.

Seen at Diss depot yard in September 2000 is N988 FWT. Despite the Yorkshire registration, this DAF SB220, built in 1996, was delivered new to Simond's. It has forty-nine-seat Ikarus bodywork, built in Hungary.

Here is a photograph of a Simond's bus at the small bus station in Diss in 2003. The vehicle, 8333 UR, is a 1992-built Dennis Dart with Plaxton Pointer thirty-four-seat body. New as number DRL35 with London Transport, it was originally registered K435 OKH.

It will soon be Christmas, at least in the opinion of the shops of central Norwich, in November 1986. Just arrived at its northern terminus, after its two-hour journey from Bury St Edmunds, is Simond's LTG 276X, a Ford R1114 with Plaxton fifty-three-seat coachwork. It was new to a Welsh operator based in Cwmbran.

Still in the livery of its previous operator, Carters of Capel St Mary, near Ipswich, JGV 929 of Simond's is seen crossing the river outside Norwich Thorpe railway station on 29 March 2012. Originally registered P192 SGV, this Optare Excel integral thirty-eight-seat bus was new to Ipswich Buses in 1997.

On 16 April 2014, Simond's BT13 YWE is loading up in Castle Meadow, Norwich, prior to departing for Diss. Purchased new less than a year earlier, the bus is a Volvo B7RLE with MCV Evolution forty-four-seat bodywork.

Coach Services of Thetford have been in business for over sixty years. Local bus routes in the Norfolk town are supplemented by longer distance ones, reaching King's Lynn and Bury St Edmunds. Back in the spring of 1985, former London Transport number DM1798 (GHM 798N) was awaiting departure from Thetford's tiny bus station, on a town service. The bus, a 1975 Daimler Fleetline with MCW body, is one of several double-deckers in the fleet.

Another ex-London Daimler Fleetline/MCW, SMU 924N, built in 1974 and numbered DM924 when on service in the capital. This one is seen at Coach Services' depot, close to Thetford town centre, spring 1985.

On the same occasion as the last two photographs, a different type of double-decker bus is seen at Coach Services' Thetford premises. GGG 306N is a Leyland Atlantean AN68A/1R with Alexander seventy-two-seat bodywork, new to Greater Glasgow Passenger Transport Executive in 1974.

Coach Services of Thetford have been using low-floor buses since the end of the last century. In 1999, at King's Lynn bus station, we see S340 SET, new to the company a year earlier. It is a Scania L94UB with Northern Ireland-built Wright bodywork, seating forty-three passengers.

More Wright bodywork is seen on CS12 BUS, an appropriate registration for a Coach Services vehicle. On 15 August 2013, this Volvo B7RLE bus, seating forty-four, is seen approaching its Thetford stopover, en route between Brandon and Bury St Edmunds.

The Optare Solo midibus has very much become the standard vehicle for bus services in the more rural parts of the country. Thetford is no exception and one is seen at the bus station in the hands of Coach Services. MW52 PYV is a thirty-three-seat example, built in 2002 and photographed on 15 August 2013.

The small Norfolk village of Caston, situated between Watton and Attleborough, was home to Colin S. Pegg, the proprietor of the local bus company. Mr Pegg started his business in 1952, taking over from a previous operator. A variety of vehicles was owned, an example being 6989 AD, seen in King's Lynn around 1974. New to Forest of Dean operator, Cottrell's of Mitcheldean, it later passed to Delaine of Bourne, Lincolnshire, prior to emigrating to Norfolk. It is an AEC Regent V of 1960, with Willowbrook bodywork.

Another AEC/Willowbrook combination with Colin S. Pegg. At the depot, *c.* 1974, is 858 GNM, a 1996-built Reliance with high-capacity bus bodywork, seating sixty-five passengers. It was new to H&C of Garston, near Watford.

Most buses in the Pegg fleet were bought second-hand. A notable exception was SPW 92N, a Leyland Atlantean AN68/2R, with dual-doored Roe bodywork, new in 1974. It is seen at the depot in Caston, displaying the unusual pink and white livery, in 1978.

On the same day as above, SPW 93N is captured on film outside the depot. This AEC Reliance, with fifty-seven-seat Duple Dominant coach body, was new to the company in 1974. After his retirement, Colin S. Pegg ceased trading as a bus company.

Towler's Coaches is based at the village of Emneth, just inside Norfolk, near the Cambridgeshire town of Wisbech. The company still exists, but concentrates on private hire and school jobs today. However, over the years, some stage services have been operated. In the spring of 1994, E905 LVE is seen departing King's Lynn bus station for Wisbech. This Optare City Pacer, based on a Volkswagen LT55 chassis, was new to Cambus as a twenty-five-seater.

Towler's have long had several double-deckers for the transport of school children. Here, at the depot in 1976, closest to the camera is LCK 752, a former Ribble Motor Services Leyland PD3/4, built in 1958 with Burlingham full-fronted body. Also visible is RBX 700, a Guy Arab IV with lowbridge Massey bodywork, new to West Wales of Tycroes, near Llanelli.

RBY 44L, in Towler's fleet, is seen in the sun at the depot in the spring of 1978. New to a Hounslow (London) operator, the coach is a 1973 Bedford VAL70, with fifty-three-seat Plaxton Elite coachwork, looking very smart indeed!

On the same beautiful fenland day as above, VHE 196 is seen alongside Towler's depot. It was new to Yorkshire Traction in 1961, when it originally bore the fleet number 1196. The bus is a Leyland PD3A/1, with Northern Counties H31/32F bodywork, unusually featuring a sliding entrance door.

Glebe Taxi Bus Ltd took advantage of the deregulation of the bus industry in the late 1980s and early 1990s, running stage carriage services based on King's Lynn. At that town's bus station in mid-1992 we see F918 YNG, a Talbot Pullman three-axle minibus, soon to take its place at a departure stance.

Glebe also utilised larger vehicles on its bus routes, as seen in this view at King's Lynn bus station in mid-1989. OCN 915R is ready to depart for Fakenham. This coach, a forty-five-seat Bedford YLQ, bodied by Plaxton, was new to Moordale, a Tyneside operator.

Cambridgeshire-based independent Emblings of Guyhirn, who recently ceased trading, ran the occasional service into King's Lynn bus station. Here, on 4 September 2012, we see TIL 5507, a Volvo B10M coach, bodied by Plaxton. The use of a 'cherished' registration has made it impossible to ascertain the origin, or further details, of this vehicle.

Another re-registered bus at King's Lynn, this time in 1982. UEX 18W was originally GML 850J, when it ran for its original owner, British Airways. This Leyland Atlantean PDR2/1R with Roe bodywork once operated between London Victoria and Heathrow Airport. In its new guise it is seen in the hands of Swaffham Coachways, a Norfolk operator that has since ceased trading.

The little market town of Harleston, in South Norfolk, was once served by Fareline, a small independent bus company, now based in Diss. In late 1983, passing the Cardinal's Hat pub, on The Thoroughfare in Harleston is Fareline's 56 GUO. Named The Royal, this coach, a 1961 Bristol MW6G with ECW thirty-nine-seat body, was new to Western National for their Royal Blue express services.

Wayland's, based just over the Suffolk border in Beccles, once ran a small number of stage carriage routes into Norfolk. At the little town of Wymondham, in the summer of 1990, D768 JUB is heading for Blofield, a village to the east of Norwich. New to Yorkshire Rider in 1986, this twenty-seat minibus is a Dormobile conversion of a Freight Rover Sherpa. Wayland's still run some infrequent bus services, mainly in Suffolk.

Neaves, a small Norfolk bus operator, have recently sold the bus service part of their business to Sanders of Holt. Until 2014, Neaves ran a couple of routes into Norwich, where PDZ 6263 was photographed in late 2000. This Leyland National was rebuilt by East Lancs in 1995 to Greenway standard for London and Country, from whom it was purchased in 1999. It was originally new to Midland Red in 1976, as NOE 562R.

Here is another Neaves vehicle, less suitable for bus services, but seen on such duties passing Norwich Thorpe railway station in summer 1990. XHE 754T is a Ford R1114 with fifty-three-seat Plaxton Supreme bodywork, new to Yorkshire coach operator, Globe of Barnsley.

Fowler's Travel, based at the Lincolnshire fenland village of Holbeach Drove, was established in 1947. Following deregulation, the company took on the busy King's Lynn to Spalding route and purchased several new buses for this task. Two examples are seen in King's Lynn bus station, in late 1993. F257 CEW and F258 CEW are both Scania K93CRB types, with Plaxton fifty-seven-seat bodies.

In the summer of 1990, Fowler's were using ex-London Country number TD36 (YPD 136Y) on the Spalding route from King's Lynn. Photographed in the bus station at the latter town, it is a Leyland Tiger with Duple Dominant forty-six-seat coachwork, fitted with folding bus-type doors.

The year 2001 saw Fowler's Travel upgrade their bus fleet with the addition of YN51 MJE, a Scania L94UB with Wright forty-three-seat bus bodywork. It is seen on arrival in King's Lynn bus station in January 2002, with decorations celebrating fifty years of the company's operations. At the time of writing, Fowler's Travel still trades, but has given up stage carriage work.

New to Wigan Buses Limited, S781 RNE was built in 1998. The bus later went to Knottybus in Staffordshire and is seen here in the hands of Millennium Freeway, a short-lived operator. The bus, a Dennis Dart with Plaxton forty-one-seat body, is seen in King's Lynn bus station, in summer 1999, on the service to Dereham via Swaffham.

Anglian Coaches was formed in 1981, as a family-owned business in Loddon, Norfolk. Soon stage carriage services became part of the company's portfolio and OWT 775M was obtained for these duties. Seen in central Norwich in spring 1985, it is an ex-West Yorkshire Road Car Company Bristol RELL6L with ECW fifty-three-seat bodywork.

Anglian Coaches later became Anglian Bus, reflecting the company's activities after gaining several Norfolk County Council tendered services since 1999. The increase in the size of the fleet prompted a move to a larger depot in Beccles, Suffolk. Fleet number 407 (YJ06 FZK) is an Optare Tempo integral forty-two-seater, seen arriving at the new bus station in Norwich, on 2 April 2009. It was previously a demonstrator for Optare.

In April 2012, Anglian Bus was purchased by the Go Ahead Group, retaining its identity. A modern fleet is operated and an example is shown here, in the form of number 307 (AU11 ESG), an Optare Versa bus with thirty-seven seats. It is crossing the River Wensum, just outside Norwich Thorpe railway station, 16 April 2014.

Same spot, same day, totally different vehicle! Anglian Bus 107 (AU62 DWL), a MAN 18.270 with Optare forty-three-seat bodywork, powered by biogas, is heading out of the city on a service to Great Yarmouth.

Anglian Bus 455 (AN61 LAN), a Scania K23OUB forty-six-seat bus, similar to many seen throughout Europe (albeit right-hand drive), has just arrived at Castle Meadow in Norwich city centre after a journey from Great Yarmouth on 16 April 2014.

Established in 1999, Konect (later known as Konectbus) was originally a coach operator, but soon began to concentrate on bus services following the gaining of Norfolk County Council contracts. The original depot was at Saham Toney, but this was soon outgrown and operations moved to Dereham. One of several former Trent Motor Traction Optare Excel forty-five-seat buses in the fleet, number 272 (S171 UAL) was captured on film in Swaffham town centre in March 2006.

Another former Trent Motor Traction bus was this forty-nine-seat Leyland National, photographed by Richard Huggins at Dereham depot on 3 March 2004. However, DAR 120T (allocated fleet number 120) was new to Eastern National, as number 1898.

On 3 March 2004, Richard Huggins also took this photo of fleet number 32 (VIB 5232) at Konect's Dereham depot. This 1982 Leyland Tiger with Plaxton Supreme coachwork was purchased from Chalkwell of Sittingbourne, Kent, in 1999. It was new as XPP 282X with Johnson of Hanslope, Buckinghamshire.

Trent Motor Traction was a good source of second-hand buses for Konect. Another vehicle that once saw service in the East Midlands was number 334 (K334 FAL), a DAF SB220 with Optare Delta forty-nine-seat body. It is seen in Dereham town centre, on a local service, in March 2005.

Konectbus was purchased by the Go Ahead Group in March 2010 and has retained its separate identity. The fleet has been greatly updated, as one can see in this picture of number 609 (SN61 CZZ), an Alexander Dennis Enviro seventy-nine-seat double-deck bus. It is arriving at Norwich Thorpe railway station on 29 March 2012, painted in a dedicated livery for route 8.

Another Konectbus Alexander Dennis Enviro at Norwich Thorpe railway station, this time on 16 April 2014. Number 603 (SN10 CFG) is in standard Konectbus fleet colours.

Number 50 (R739 XRV) in the Konectbus fleet is, at the time of writing, the only open-top bus owned. It was acquired from Southern Vectis, the Isle of Wight operator in the Go Ahead Group, in 2014. Hugh Madgin photographed this Volvo Olympian/Northern Counties bus on Beach Road in Cromer, on 29 August 2015.

The history of Sanders Coaches dates back to 1975. The company, still independent today, is based at the small North Norfolk town of Holt and bus routes are operated throughout the local area, reaching Cromer, Norwich and King's Lynn. The old livery style is seen here at the depot on 13 June 1998, through the lens of Richard Huggins's camera. The main subject of the photograph is D601 RGJ, a Bedford YMT with Plaxton fifty-three-seat bus bodywork, new to Epsom Coaches. Alongside is re-registered Plaxton coach SJI 1621.

Sanders Coaches-owned M971 CVG, a Mercedes 711D minibus with Plaxton bodywork containing twenty-five coach seats, seen in the layover area of King's Lynn bus station, April 1997. Sanders bought the vehicle new.

The new bus station in Norwich forms the backdrop to this photograph of DAF SB220/Optare Delta bus R31 GNW, seen in the hands of Sanders Coaches in March 2006. New to Speedlink for airport operations, it has since been exported to Ireland.

W261 CDN was also new to an airport operator, this time at Luton, Bedfordshire. Seen in the latest livery of Sanders Coaches at Castle Meadow, Norwich, on 2 April 2009, it is a DAF SB220 with East Lancashire bus bodywork.

In Sanders' all-over orange livery, thirty-three-seat Optare Solo midibus AU03 HWS is seen in Cromer's small bus station on 29 August 2015. The bus was new to Anglian Coaches. Thanks to Hugh Madgin for allowing use of this photograph.

Appropriately named Goliath, OU05 KLA of Sanders Coaches is seen in Castle Meadow, Norwich, on 16 April 2014. This three-axle Volvo B9TL, with East Lancashire bodywork was new to Berkshire operator Weavaway. It will certainly provide sufficient capacity on the service to the North Norfolk coast.

On 16 April 2014, in Castle Meadow, Norwich, we see Sanders Coaches' YN06 NXR. This smart-looking Scania L94UB, with Wright forty-three-seat bodywork, was new to Reading Transport. The bus is nearing its terminus, the city's bus station, at the end of a long journey from Holt on route 45.

Another well-turned-out Sanders Coaches bus, again sourced from Reading Transport. YN54 AFV is a Scania N94UD with East Lancashire bodywork designed to seat eighty passengers. Photographed on 16 April 2014, at Castle Meadow, Norwich.

Norfolk Green, founded in 1996, rapidly expanded to become the predominant operator in the King's Lynn area. Back in March 1997, when First Eastern Counties ruled the roost in King's Lynn, one of Norfolk Green's Mercedes L608D/Alexander minibuses will soon set out on a local service. D511 NWG was new to Yorkshire Traction in 1986.

It is mid-2000 and Norfolk Green's buses have grown slightly bigger. F401 XWR is a Mercedes 811D with Optare StarRider thirty-three-seat bodywork, new to ceased Hertfordshire operator Welwyn-Hatfield Line. The bus will shortly leave King's Lynn bus station for the nearby village of Magdelen.

Another bus in the Norfolk Green fleet purchased from a Hertfordshire operator. G624 WPB was once used to run the Reg's Coaches Hertford town service. This 1990 Dennis Dart with Duple thirty-nine-seat bodywork is seen in King's Lynn bus station in March 1997.

King's Lynn bus station is once again the venue of this photograph taken on 15 March 2008. The subject is Norfolk Green's J526 GCD, a Dennis Dart with Alexander Dash bodywork, seating forty-one passengers. By the time of the photograph, fleet numbers had been introduced. Number 226 was new to Stagecoach South.

In 2011 First Group pulled out of King's Lynn, selling their services to Norfolk Green. The Coasthopper routes to Hunstanton and along the North Norfolk coast became very popular, especially during the holiday season. By then, Norfolk Green had begun naming their buses. Optare Solo 313 (YJ09 LBE) was called 'Tony, Tom and Bob too', after the company's first regular Coasthopper drivers when the service was started in 1996. King's Lynn bus station, 4 September 2012.

One of many Optare Solos in the Norfolk Green fleet, number 618 (MX54 WMJ), was painted in a special livery to remember the long-gone Midland & Great Northern Railway. The M&GN once ran from South Lincolnshire, through Norfolk Green territory, to the North Norfolk Coast. The thirty-three-seat bus, new to a Derbyshire operator, is seen in central Norwich on 2 April 2009.

Norfolk Green's *Miranda Glynn*, number 206 (P195 SGV) is seen in King's Lynn bus station, about to go on service, on 10 November 2010. This Optare Excel was formerly number 195 of the Ipswich Buses fleet.

Norfolk Green operated several double-deck buses, including number 10 (LV52 HHP), named *John Colton*. New to East London Buses, this Dennis Trident/Alexander bus is seen arriving in King's Lynn bus station, past the Lord Kelvin pub, 4 September 2012.

In December 2013, after the retirement of the proprietor, Norfolk Green was sold to the Stagecoach Group. Upon purchase, the only change was the addition of the corporate numbering system. At King's Lynn bus station, on 20 March 2015, number 13988 *Frances Burney* (YJ03 UMK) is in the parking area. This DAF/Optare Spectra double-decker was new to Reading Transport.

Stagecoach Coasthopper 39898 *Sir William Hoste* (GX07 BAU), is a rare vehicle, which did not last long with its new owners. This Iris Agora Line forty-four-seat bus was built for Norse, the erstwhile operators of park-and-ride services in Norwich. The bus is seen at Castle Meadow, in its home city, 16 April 2014. Research indicates that Sir William Hoste was a famous Norfolk sea captain.

Norfolk Green certainly liked the products of the Yorkshire-based bodybuilder Optare. Named after a former Hunstanton dignitary, Henry le Strange, YJ06 YSP is an Optare Tempo saloon, new to Marshall's of Sutton-on-Trent, Nottinghamshire. It is seen in King's Lynn bus station carrying Stagecoach fleet number 25120, on 20 March 2015.

On the same occasion as the above photo, Stagecoach number 25270 *Sox the Dog* (YJ10 EYC) is an Optare Versa saloon, bought new by Norfolk Green. It is loading up in King's Lynn bus station on a local route to North Wootton. According to the small print on the bus, Sox is a friendly Staffordshire terrier who helps out in the RSPCA's Hunstanton shop.

Not long after the takeover, Stagecoach introduced a new livery to the Norfolk Green fleet. It is seen here applied to number 10052 *Johnny Douglas* (SN12 EHM), an Alexander Dennis Enviro double-decker. King's Lynn bus station, 20 March 2015.

Sadly, in May 2015, the decision was made to incorporate the Norfolk Green buses into the Stagecoach East fleet. The green colours will soon be replaced by those seen elsewhere in the Stagecoach Group. On 20 March 2015, a foretaste of what was to come is seen in King's Lynn bus station. Number 34639 (GX54 DWK), a standard Dennis Dart SLF, has just been transferred to Norfolk from Stagecoach South.

Long before the demise of Norfolk Green, Stagecoach buses were occasionally to be seen in King's Lynn bus station. These were operated by Viscount, the Peterborough-based operations of the former Cambus concern. Lettered Stagecoach Viscount, number 590 (S590 BCE) in that fleet is a coach-seated Volvo Olympian/Alexander double-decker. It is seen leaving King's Lynn bus station in summer 1999.

We have witnessed the demise of First Group and Norfolk Green on the King's Lynn–Hunstanton service. Now there is competition again! A new company, trading as Lynxbus, are using a small fleet of Optare Tempo saloons, such as this thirty-four-seater ex-demonstrator, seen loading up in King's Lynn bus station, 20 March 2015.